On Low Gap Road

a collection of poetry and vignettes

On Low Gap Road

a collection of poetry and vignettes

Kyle Robert Alvey

RABBIT
HOUSE
PRESS
rabbithousepress.com

Part IV: Mamaw

Part V: Life Together

Dedication

This volume is in memory of Robert Oscar Haight and Edna Sims Haight, my Papaw and Mamaw. They passed away when I was in high school. I wish I had known them as an adult. I think we would have much in common. Also, in memory of their infant child and my uncle David Haight, who passed in 2018. Lastly, this collection is dedicated to my mother and sister, who do everything for me.

Robert and Edna Haight standing at Berea College in the late 1940s

Introduction

I am writing this in the summer of 2023, after my first year of teaching high school in the same school where my grandparents ended their teaching careers. My Papaw taught Agriculture and sponsored the Future Farmers of America (FFA). My Mamaw taught Home-Economics. By the time I came around (1996), both had been retired from teaching for multiple decades. Their farm was their life, which I shared in during trips from Owensboro, KY to the Greenup Co. KY area. My memories of childhood visits include exploring the trees, fields, and creeks of the farm, walking through "His garden" (Papaw's), watching tv in the living room with my grandparents in their armchairs, fishing in the pond, searching through the assorted outbuildings filled with years of my grandparents' bits and ends, reading in the swing, and enjoying great home cooking in the mornings, afternoons, and evenings.

I hope for this volume to provide a purposeful reimagination of my childhood with a focus on those around me, be a vigorous and honest reflection on where and who I come from, connect the two sides of Kentucky which split my life, and attempt to visualize how my Mamaw and Papaw lived when no one was watching, especially me. It is my hope that these representations of Kentucky life in the 20th and 21st centuries will bring back memories for readers, create bonds between generations, and honor a life of simplicity, work, and family.

The poetry explores aspects of my childhood living on a tobacco farm outside of Owensboro and visiting family in Greenup County. It creates a representation of what life on the farm in Eastern KY may have been like for my Mamaw and Papaw based on stories, my own observations, and details of the farm still left behind. I hope to depict my grandparents as the hardworking people I knew them to be, while creating them anew as characters I can dig into and rediscover how they viewed the world. All faults in my depictions are my own, but I am confident that I am coming close to doing them justice, while also revealing some inner thoughts I have about them, which I like to believe they believed.

The vignettes are attempts at characterizing Mamaw and Papaw in ways people of Eastern Kentucky will recognize. My childhood came along 20 years after they retired from their teaching careers. My time spent on Low Gap consisted of watching TV in the many recliners they had in their front room, walking along the fields and around the pond, visiting with family, and eating delicious gravy and biscuits in the morning, ham sandwiches in the afternoon, and a warm dinner in the evening. Those experiences and memories showed me another part of Kentucky life.

I hope to make the connection between the different types of people who live in Kentucky. Our differences, when they are positive, make us stronger. We should all recognize where and who we come from and do our best to keep memories and narratives alive. This is my part in putting the Kentucky most special to me on the page. I intend to do so throughout my life.

Robert Haight (Papaw) taking his dogs along on his tractor, circa 1990s.

Part I

The Tobacco Farm

Kyle Robert Alvey

the valley

Western Kentucky shies away from Appalachia
Proud of the flat fields of corn
Dispersed beside currents of the Ohio
Which has turned brown

Where Daviess County meets Mclean
The road of my childhood leads off
To the left

Blacktop climbs up sudden hills
And curves around silos
Passing my childhood house
It descends

The valley opens up, stretching
From left to right
North to south
Of the diagonal road

Field touches field
Color bleeds and the smell of earth
Is the freshest you can find
The city is far

The valley is where my armies gathered
Where my mind grew from each new book
And adventures I dreamed

The valley is the root of it all
Because it was my first home

Kyle Robert Alvey

tobacco

A sturdy plant that requires
More steps than any other
To end up in stores and homes
Lastly into lungs

Small green plants in Styrofoam trays
Float on algae covered water
Waiting for laborers
Who cultivate

Plant in the summer
With the fiercest sun above
Row after row
Field after field

Conversations happen
In planting season
They continue
Until brown leaves are stripped away

And sent off…

Kyle R. Alvey

childhood home

If the size of a house mattered
My life would be stunted
But the love my family had for me
And my sister
Made our circumstances

White paneling on the outside
Cracks by the roof of the carport
Allow raccoons to come in

A field and valley touch the side yard
A red barn stands nearby
Barely
Beyond other barns and buildings
I explore

Inside, cramped furniture
Wall to wall
Perhaps why I prefer
To fill a room
China cabinets
And seasonal decorations
Tell small little stories

A deer head and bunk beds
A wet and damp basement
A concrete patio
Leading to a swing

We slept, we ate, we watched tv
We fought, we talked, we learned
We grew
In that house

Kyle R. Alvey

the red barn

Even as a child the roof was mostly missing
Leaving the contents exposed to the elements
Especially when rain crashed down
And tornados threatened to form

I am not sure when it was painted
But before my memory starts
Which is more than a quarter century
The red had peeled and peeled

The important bit, the rafters,
Allowed one to climb up and up
I only went to the very top once
When no one knew

On Low Gap Road

That is where tobacco plants
Speared on wooden sticks
Were left out to dry
To reach a certain quality
To be determined in paper and pipes

The red barn housed many things
Some discarded forever
Others waiting to be used

I am one of the things
The red barn did not keep

Kyle R. Alvey

apple trees and cows

Opposite of that barn was the grazing field
Where cows waited for us
To toss apples over the fence

I would hold out an apple
Let the thick gray tongue touch me
As sturdy teeth bit and chewed
I was fascinated by their eyes
Which lit up as they ate

Three apple trees stood beside our house
One, the leader, stood strong and tall
One, the runt, had a trunk you could wrap
Your hand around
The last was squat and many-limbed
Which we climbed often
To view birds' nests
And throw mushy fruit
To the madding and spotted crowd

tractors

Mechanical creatures
Of intricate parts
And giant wheels
Towered high above me

Those creatures powered up
And moved with incredible speeds
In my young eyes
I respected them for their efforts

Out in a far-off field, discing up the soil
Close by, delivering rolled hay
Even closer still, and I climb up to the seat
Given a proper view

Once one rolled out of control
Because I turned the steering wheel
As it sat in neutral at the top of the hill
My great-uncle sprinted and climbed it
Calming the mechanical beast, everything has dangers

Kyle R. Alvey

a mama cat

I learned to love cats early on
With their different coats, colors
And personalities

I cannot remember her
But my oldest pictures show
Me with a wide grin
And her peeking in

I have a soft spot for calicos
Maybe because they remind me of her
In some deep subconscious area

She had many litters and prowled wide
I am not sure how and when she left us
But being a farm cat has its ups and downs
Dangers all around
But food and children to play with count for something

13

Her most important lessons for me
To love the most vulnerable
To cherish each small kitten
To take care of animals
Especially the abandoned
And the ones no one wants

Original home built on Low Gap Road in 1954

Part II

The Garden and the Table

Kyle R. Alvey

in the east

Hours and miles we would travel
To reach the garden and the house
Down a sloped gravel driveway
With small fields on either side

The white house, with porch and covered carport
And array of barns and buildings
Which housed the discards of decades of farming
In front, mirroring back home,
Three sturdy apple trees, growing green fruit instead of
Red

The farm sprawls and connects with a gravel road
Which I spent my childhood walking
Often barefoot
If the weather allowed

I grew up hearing passed down wisdom
When the month has an "R"
It is time
To the put the shoes back on

On Low Gap Road

To the right was a covered swing
Where I would sit alone
Kept company with a book
Or one of the many Jack Russell terriers
From the enclosed doghouse

Beyond the trees in front was the pond
Filled with large bass and who knows
What else
The cows that used to live here were long gone
By my time

Behind the house, down a sharp yet smooth hill
Is where it lay
Covering an acre or less

Kyle R. Alvey

corn

Being lost in a cornfield is one thing
It is another to stroll among four rows

The adventure lies between the plants
But still, you cannot lose your way

By my childhood, rows and rows had
Slimmed down to a simple four

Taller than me by far
I looked up at the gleaming ears
And adored the gold

green beans

Low to the ground with green leaves
And wrapped in tight coils
I always reached out to touch
Consistently enwrapped by the fuzzy
Green shells

Nature amazingly creates green things
Then makes a different hue
Once you think you know
You see another iteration at your feet
I adore it

I grew up with home grown green beans
And those from a can
Of course, one is better than the other
But that's because of the people who prepare it

Green beans from a can
can still be good
good enough
But there is nothing like directly from the soil
And when you wipe off the dry dirt
To prep them for the bowl

potatoes

With so many ways to prepare them
Everyone loves the tuber root
Which hides below the surface
As it grows

Walking among the potatoes
It is important to tread softly
Especially if you were me
And pretended they slept

Rows of these grew in somber slumber
And this part of the garden
Always felt inviting
As if it recognizing I meant well

When the season came around
So did the time to dig with a gentle hand
Pull them into the light
Providing starch for hungry mouths
And mashed up for the family

Kyle R. Alvey

lettuce and cabbage

These green orbs

      Lying like discarded

            Rolling heads

I would watch as a worm climbed the slope
Of a head of cabbage
Or down the curve
Of a head of lettuce

It is important to tend to these
To keep the weeds away
Who wish to strangle the life
From these manifestations
Of nature

Side by side one would not believe
The different tastes in these similar
Vegetables
Boiled lettuce is ruined
Boiled cabbage a staple

Those who perfected the cooking craft
Which we depend on everyday
Learned through trial and error
To separate cabbage from lettuce

Kyle R. Alvey

a vegetable medley

Struggling for life in the same dirt
Drinking the same water
A vegetable medley spread from path to creek
From the base of a hill to another creek fork

In one row onions
Another a line of broccoli
Cauliflower plants enjoying the shade
From leafy cucumber vines
Bright and vibrant peppers
Next to a growing group of radishes
Squash nearly stacked atop another
With zucchini resting steps away
Move and see the turnips
In their strange purplish color
Beets and peas together
Trying to share
All neatly finished
With a row of vivid pumpkins

And an assortment of growing watermelons
Natural flavors growing up together
Not knowing their true purpose
They were content in the warm sun
And the sudden drops of rain

Years later I can still see it
Still breathe that air
But memories can be faulty
And they fail to write things down

Kyle R. Alvey

simple fences and the yield

The first design was made of twine
With interwoven patterns meant to faze
Passing deer
Next came wire, barbed and twisted
This protected the garden
And potential growth

Last came electric wire
Able to zap and sting
If I ever reached out to touch it
I would quickly stumble back
I was taught to raise and lower
To climb over or burrow under

Fences are important for gardens
Beyond simple protection
They lend themselves to form shape
In this case a wide square
Of the yield produced within

The electric fence sings and hums
And the vegetables sit to listen
Waiting, though they do not know it
To be picked

presented on the table

All of this fresh produce
Has been sliced and cut
Boiled and mashed
Steamed and dried
Cubed and diced

She has been working all day
Preparing for supper
Because everyone is coming around tonight
And will come hungry

She bakes a ham
And bread to accompany
In bowls go the vegetables

For dessert is pie or a cake
And when everyone has finished
Piled up the plates
They thank her by doing the dishes

29

When she finally gets to recline in her chair
With all of us spread out across a landscape of chairs,
floor, and couches
She feels content
Because the fruits of her labor were delicious

And everyone knows it

Remnants of Bob and Edna's cellar where they stored all home grown canned produce.

Robert's old smokehouse where he pestered the hogs and cured hams and bacon.

Robert Haight enjoying some home grown corn outside, circa 1985

Part III

Papaw

Kyle R. Alvey

his hands

Rough and calloused
Stained with the darkest dirt
That comes from years of work

Nails kept short by need
Wrinkles running here and there
Come from years of life

Scars of cuts and distortions of bruises
Veins visible within the palms
That comes from years of stress

Strong and steady
Durable and capable
That comes from years of experience

35

His hands provided
For us

I wish I had been smart enough
To say thanks

Kyle R. Alvey

lost creek

Hollers rise and fall
Where moonshine stills were commonplace
In days past

In the far extremes of the county
Where small creeks bubble along
And fields lie fallow

Is where he came from, isolated
From the intensity of others
Among the quiet

The same-named creek moves
By and by even today
But maybe then it roared

The place of origin remembers the name
Of the family
It bears like a brand

Even though we hardly visit
And old stones go unturned
Time will always go and

Still, we know the way to the home
I imagine him as a child
Reared on lost creek

Kyle R. Alvey

who he came from

In boyhood there was work
Keeping a small farm alive
In a time when commercialization
Reared its ugly head

His parents taught him what to value
And who
In a time when it was common
To value the wrong things

His mother and his father
Were of an Appalachian generation
That meant
Put in more than you take

In simple dress, in a simple house
With a delicate beauty
That went unlooked for
Because farming took the eyes

They taught him to read and enjoy
Storytelling
At least I imagine so
Since I was taught

They taught him to do the difficult
The tender and the raw
To love when necessary
To help the ground produce
Proudly

siblings

A brother and a sister
Who never traveled far beyond
The homestead

They were his constants in this world
Of change

Hearts that were shaped like diamonds
From pressure of ground
And of fear
Which marked the times

I know little of them, which pains me
But my imagination is free
To place three siblings walking arm-in-arm
Laughing together
And enjoying each other
Whether or not that ever happened

Does not matter

an early outlook

Perspectives on life are possible
At birth, if nurtured well
Here are some thoughts on what
I think he knew

Education is the solution in the face of deadly
ignorance.
Voices should be valued, even if we don't listen.
Change happens from within and without.
Impoverished people deserve help.
Indifference is worse than pure evil.
We have more in common with our neighbors than
they want us to believe.
Creating is part of life.
It is our responsibility to provide opportunities for
those who come next.
Nature should be celebrated and kept pure.
History shapes our future, so we should know it.
Deadly ignorance is rampant around us, in the guise
of good and shiny things.

war service

Papaw enlisted the day after Pearl Harbor
Like thousands of young people across the country
Seeing the Pacific for the first time
Must have been a powerful moment
But war is a difficult subject
I would much rather he could have traveled
To new parts of the globe with educational groups
As I have gotten to do
Instead of taking part in war
But he did that, so I could take my trips
This is something I find it difficult to think about
Hundreds of thousands of people died
So I could be here
He would have been in the first waves of troops
To storm mainland Japan
If they had not dropped the bombs
And I would not exist

43

War is a complex thing
And those who run the world
Never die in those fights

berea college

after service

a return to college awaited

and so did she

Robert and Edna Haight graduating from Berea College, circa 1948

Edna Haight (Mamaw) making dumplings in her kitchen, circa early 1990s

Part IV

Mamaw

her hands

I remember them as wrinkled things
Resting in her lap or submerged in soapy water
I sat and held them
Seeing the veins so close to the surface
As if they were going to break free
She bruised easily
As people tend to do in old age
And I would trace purple smudges
Wishing they would go away
Being too young to know she had earned them
By living a long, fulfilled life
Her hands were strong
Her hands were gentle
Her hands are the support of my family

tompkinsville

Another small Kentucky town has fallen
Into severe disrepair
Or last I've heard

Born and raised there, Mamaw never went back
To stay
I do not remember her ever talking about it

So far away it may as well be in another state
In Tennessee or beyond
A place I have never been

Yet a place that if it had never been
I would never be
Crucial to my life equation

Perhaps I shall visit, though nothing she knew
Remains the same
But I can imagine it

Kyle R. Alvey

who she came from

They seem too elusive now
Like shadows and forms
That hover just beyond
My range of sight
I have learned their names and ages
Most else remains vague
They had to have loved her
I knew her in her oldest years
And she was still vibrant
I imagine in her younger days
She loved them just the same
I imagine it pained her to move away
To start a new life beyond
The horizon of her home
My own mother barely got to know them
So, all I have are retold memories
Which fade and fade and fade
But it is something worth holding on to
And putting down on paper

siblings

I never met them.
I have only seen them
In photos. Depicting them
In a hazy blur. But still, I see them
For who they were.

Kyle R. Alvey

an early outlook

Again, I picture her outlook on life
Largely shaped my own
That it was my inheritance
Enshrined in wisdom and heritage
So, I pull my own apart
To find remains of hers
And know how she loved
She loved fiercely and deeply
But it was a love that was earned
By fulfilling a role
She loved without question
But it was a love that pushed
One to be better
She loved without regrets
But she had some of her own
Because that's what life is
She loved without error
Not in fragments or with cracks
She loved all she knew
And that which she saw

leaving

She left her home to forge a new path
On a cold morning she closed a door behind her
And stepped into a new life
Though it pained her, it felt right
The air constricted around her
Threatening to force fear
But she held firm against it
And left her first home

berea college

she thought a degree

      was the bulk of what lay ahead

            but everything waited before her

55

On Low Gap Road

Robert and Edna Haight, early marriage circa 1947

Part V

Life Together

Kyle R. Alvey

the farm

On Low Gap where creeks sing
And trees sway in gentle winds
There lies the family homestead
Where he and she built a life together
And many lives after

With fields from left to right
That raise grass to become hay
For cattle that sound on a moonless night
And a pond filled with bass
Accompanied by small blue gill

A collection of barns, stalls, and pens
House chickens, pigs, and even once
A brilliant peacock
That stood out amongst the gray

59

White gravel shines under the blazing sun
Which guides on the path down
To the house and farm they built together
And the life contained within

Kyle R. Alvey

the house

Their bedrooms across the hall from each other
Down a long hall from the kitchen
Which they call the utility closet and pantry
Enclosed by the back door
Where you can crush pop cans
A sliding door to the bedroom
Next to the one with the piano
The boys' bedroom with small bunk beds
With a paired desk and chair
The kitchen and table
Where meals unfold
Finally, the living room
With low to the floor TV
Where we all watched Wheel of Fortune
And David Letterman
Mamaw and Papaw's house
Will always be in my mind

teaching

Something innate brought them both to teaching
Perhaps the same thing
That brought them together

I can still encounter a student of theirs
If I go out searching
And they remember their wisdom

Papaw taught agriculture
The science and magic
Of making plants grow

Mamaw taught home ec
How to run a household
And not let it run you

Their teaching complemented each other
Reflecting their daily lives
They lived as they taught

Kyle R. Alvey

losing a child

I would have had another uncle
But he did not survive
By the time I came around
It was never mentioned
If it had ever been
Such a subject is taboo
Or at least not appropriate
To discuss at the dinner table
Before my Mamaw died
She told my mom, her daughter
That she would get to hold
Her little baby again soon
And that softens the pain of losing her

My own lack of faith
Does not affect hers

the three boys

Mamaw and Papaw
Had three boys

They slept in the bunk room
Like boys do

They punched and rolled
And were rowdy

The boys roamed the farm
And were put to work

They fished in the pond
And went off to school

They all stayed nearby
And cared for their parents

We have lost one now
Forever incomplete

and two girls

I imagine Mamaw was happy
To have her girls
Who may normally have been a calm
In the calamity of farm life
But my mother likely made nothing easy
As she will gladly tell you
They worked in the garden and the fields
Fed the cattle and the pigs
All of the children, boys and girls
Toiled alongside their parents
In the blistering Appalachian sun
Which is closer to Earth
It seems

the haights

By a final tally
The Haights were a family of seven

Let us watch
As they come together for a portrait

In the back
Edna and Bob stand arm to arm

To the sides
The brothers D-, R-, and D-

In the front
The sisters B- and S-

They range in ages
Mirroring the longevity of the family

All look to the camera
And we capture them forever and tomorrow

Homeplace nowadays

Part VI

Who Comes Next

Kyle R. Alvey

all these grandchildren

We began to emerge over forty years ago
I am the last who entered the fray
We are rarely all together
In fact, I could not tell you the last time
All of us crammed in together
To force a smile for a flash
We are scattered, spread across the country
With families, and jobs, and dreams of our own
We share a sacred bond
That stems from Robert and Edna Haight
If they could see all these grandchildren
And the things that they have done
I believe they would celebrate and mourn
Would praise and sigh
All of us are trying
That's what it was all for

a family photo

One of the only times most of us were together
We gathered in front of the house
For a family photo

Cousins with aunts and uncles
All clustered around Papaw and Mamaw
Who held her great-grandchild

We had never taken a family photo like this before
And we have not since
A memory means more when it has little company

We all smiled together, knowing who we were
And we can all still remember
But now we are missing

A series of photos can be looked through quickly
One after the other after the other
But this is one I pause on

Because I remember that day, the heat from the sun
Basking my family together
In a photo

her funeral

What I remember most is the hesitation
I had going up to the casket
While others stood in the traditional line
Shaking hands, hugging, and even laughing
I felt cold
Death is something that we are born knowing about
Though not understanding
In a moment I understood with clarity
Mamaw was gone and I would not see her again
If I ever fall in love that person will not meet her
If I ever have children, they will not know her
Not only will she be gone
She will have been gone so long
That it's hard to remember
I did eventually go to the casket
And probably breaking a funeral home rule
Put my hand on hers
She felt cold

I wished I could take that icy feeling away
And while I did not remove it from her
I took part of it with me
As I lifted my part of the casket
Pulling on the metal rod
I understood what it means to lose
A loved one
I bore the pall

his funeral

My hesitation had been replaced with urgency
Let's get this over with
So, I do not have to sit here and pretend
That everything is alright
Perhaps it was the beginning of maturity
But I did not cry at his funeral
Nor did I feel an icy diamond forming inside
Instead, I felt tired
As if I had been working nonstop for days
Which perhaps I had
At least mentally
When you have a couple like Mamaw and Papaw
Married for decades
As one passes away it becomes a tragedy
When the other goes
It is a reunion
I was saddened of course
But I knew they were together again
In death
Whatever that may mean

the cemetery

There are several places in this world where my feet know exactly where to go the paths I have walked across the dirt become memories and I trace them with each step the cemetery where they are buried is one of these places and will be for as long as I live they are buried on the flat top of a hill which descends in all directions beyond are trees flapping in the wind a town is far enough away that you cannot hear it the sun shines bright here it feels good a natural embrace that tries to comfort there are always people nearby who need that comfort sometimes I need that warm touch I know my way around here but I wish I did not have to

a reflection

When I hear the titles "Mamaw and Papaw"
I am immediately transported back to Low Gap Road
I vividly remember large pieces of my childhood
I remember them and their voices
I remember the way they chose to live
Surrounding themselves with family and hard work
I remember their hands and their eyes
I remember nights spent in a bunk bed
I remember mornings at their kitchen table
I remember casting a reel into their pond
I remember walking in the garden
I remember wiping dust and grime
From bits and ends scattered across the farm
I remember seeing snakes and dogs
I remember driving down the gravel driveway
I remember sitting in the swing
I remember walking up to get the mail
I remember being all together to watch tv
I remember cleaning dishes

I remember sneaking ice cream
I remember being awake late at night
I remember afternoon naps
I remember who they were
I remember where I come from
And I know
Who I come from and can guess on the
Why

On Low Gap Road

Robert and Edna Haight sitting at the dinner table in their kitchen, circa 1980s

Vignettes

A Talk with Papaw About Mamaw &

A Talk with Mamaw About Papaw

Mamaw passed away in the summer of 2011, as I was about to begin my sophomore year of high school. I spent a lot of that summer in Greenup, bouncing between family members' houses as my mother stayed with Mamaw at the nursing home and eventually the hospice center. One night I stayed alone with Papaw. We had been to visit her, and we came back to the house together. The sun was winding down, but it was not quite time for bed. We did not sit in the living room, instead choosing to sit at the kitchen table. Papaw warmed up a cup of coffee, and if I remember I drank a can of soda. We did not say much of anything, choosing to look at our respective drinks in silence. Eventually, we both went off to bed. I was incapable of saying what needed to be said. Papaw did not need any insights from an inexperienced high schooler.

Now for the power of the imagination and fiction. In this very short piece, I am stepping in as I am now for my high school self.

I clear my throat. I am temporarily overwhelmed by the smells and sights of this old kitchen table. But I have a purpose here and push forward.

"She loves you," I start.

He looks up at me, surprise in his stern and tired features.

"She loves you just as she did when you met at Berea."

He looks down at his coffee cup, stained on the inside from years of use.

I envision this conversation as long and deep. But it's already over. I've said what he needed to hear. Somehow, all those years ago I did not have the knowledge or skill to say it.

My Papaw liked to pick and pull-on people. He could easily get anyone of us angry and frustrated. I think it was part of how he kept himself entertained. I also think it was his way of still trying to shape us. Thick skin comes in handy in the real world, as he well knew. He wanted us to have callouses. Mine are still there.

Mamaw and I sit side-by-side on the swing, gently rocking back and forth. One of the Jack Russell Terriers lays on the ground nearby, biting into a stick. I watch as her sharp teeth peel off bark and splinters.

"He loves you," says Mamaw.

It's the first thing she's said since she came out to join me, after I ran from the kitchen table.

"He loves you very much."

We continue pushing off the ground with our feet, swinging gently. The paint of the arm rail is chipped, and I run a finger down a distortion in the wood.

"It doesn't feel like it," I say.

"Love isn't always easy," she looks around us, over at the house, and back behind at the smokehouse. "In fact, it rarely is. He wants you to be able to take care of yourself in the times ahead."

I don't respond to that. I look back down at the dog, who is looking back with a tilted head.

"Love is a challenge," she drapes an arm around me. "We all struggle with getting it right." We continue the gentle rocking. I can feel myself calming down and my anger easing away.

"Let's go get the mail," we stand up together and walk along the gravel, the little dog following behind.

I Can Always Go See It

It is late afternoon, the beginning of May. I turn twenty-seven in less than a week. I have just finished the school day. It was a good day. The students and I are in good spirits, since the school year is rapidly drawing to a close. It has been a tough year, but extremely rewarding. My first in a high school classroom as the one in charge. I can still feel the exhaustion that will take some time to go away.

I am getting dinner with my mother tonight, but she's busy in the meantime. I have time to kill. As I drive down US 23, I make a decision. I turn right onto Route 2. This road is one of the curviest I have ever been on. It winds round and round, following Appalachian remnants beside the Little Sandy. I turn up "Sweet Emotion" by Aerosmith.

I turn left onto Low Gap Road. I drive along a steep curve, and then Mamaw and Papaw's house comes into view. The pond shimmers in the sunlight that still has several hours yet. The house sits quietly. I turn and park at the top of the long gravel driveway.

I sit for a moment, remembering many things, but still in the context of my day at school. I think of what they would say if they knew I was teaching in the same school they closed out their own teaching careers. I wistfully think about what they would say if they could be here beside me, knowing all I know. I think about how I could stop here anytime I wished, simply to remember.

I back out of the driveway and head towards home, switching over to a podcast. I let myself fall into the news stories they are discussing and keep driving away from the past. But I look back in the rearview mirror. And I always will.

Epilogue

This collection is two feet standing in the past. In an aim to pull that past forward, I include this speech. My sister got married in the beginning of summer, representing everything about the future, new people coming into my life and ones joining our family. I wish Mamaw and Papaw could have been there, and I know they were, through my eyes and the eyes of our family.

June 22nd, 2023, Louisville Kentucky

excerpt from my best man's speech at my sister's wedding

First, I want to comment on how teacher heavy this wedding is, to the point where I should be getting PD (personal development) hours for this. If you're a teacher, please stand for a brief round of applause.

From an early age, Megan and I were taught to value education. For us, it's been our way up and out. CJ is very much the same way, as I'm sure most of us here are, so thank you to our parents for instilling that need to grow and learn.

As I am an English teacher, my speech does have a thesis. Thesis: The value I have for Megan and CJ stems from the memories we have shared, good and bad, and the love that reflects our personalities, our characters, and our movements from the past to the future.

Megan and CJ are high-achieving people… But these are not what I consider to be their highest achievements. Megan and CJ's biggest achievements are each other: they have managed to find someone in this wide world that complements the other and creates a whole. They are strong individuals but have created an even stronger marriage. Today we're putting what has already existed for a long time on paper.

They are my siblings, and we will always be there for each other. Every year we create more memories that make getting together more fun.

Here is a crash course on some of those memories:

The first time we went to Red River Gorge we climbed the steep trail to the top of Natural Bridge. I thought I was dying. We reach the top and come around a corner, where the sky lifts are. I, of course, turn to confront Megan about the existence of these. She gives me a shit-eating grin and a shrug. Next time we went, I paid the bill for the sky lifts.

Megan's cat Arya once potentially witnessed a murder from her window perch. I was not convinced when she told the police she didn't see anything. Sometimes I wonder if she is the real killer.

CJ and I were once tasked to go pick up the food in Ashland. I got rear-ended by an elderly couple. Turns out we had friends in common.

One time, Megan donated blood and asked me to help her get home. I helped her stagger past the sea of frat and sorority houses. I think I got a glimpse of other people's college realities.

The three of us have cats that mirror our personalities. Arya: the princess. Eugene: the quiet but intent observer. And I have two, Bilbo and Sammy, so interpret that how you will.

When I was asked to be best man, we had spent the day at the Greenup County lawnmower races.

While we were all at UK, we would do Sunday family dinners. I miss being able to do that. Thanks to FaceTime we get to talk every day. Isn't technology wonderful?

Without getting into any examples, we have a song that we often sing called I'm going to hell when I die. We're raunchy.

And lastly, here is a list of places where either I, Megan, or CJ are banned. An elementary school playground in Owensboro KY. That's the end of the list because CJ and I aren't banned anywhere. Please raise a glass to Megan and CJ!